METEORIC FLOWERS

ELIZABETH WILLIS

WESLEYAN UNIVERSITY PRESS

METEORIC FLOWERS

MIDDLETOWN, CONNECTICUT

WESLEYAN POETRY

Published by Wesleyan University Press
Middletown, CT 06459
www.wesleyan.edu/wespress

Design and composition by Quemadura
Printed on acid-free, recycled paper
in the United States of America

Library of Congress Cataloging-in-Publication Data
Willis, Elizabeth.
Meteoric flowers / Elizabeth Willis.
p. cm. — (Wesleyan poetry)
ISBN-13: 978-0-8195-6849-6
ISBN-10: 0-8195-6849-X
I. Title. II. Series.
PS3573.I456523M47 2006
811′.54—dc22
2005034679

Contents

CANTO.

VERSES OMITTED BY MISTAKE.

CANTO.

A poem is a meteor. WALLACE STEVENS

CANTO.

THE SIMILITUDE OF
THIS GREAT FLOWER

These vines are trim, I take them down. I have my mother's features in my heart, the darkest gem, tripping in the tar, an affinity for Iceland. The world is clanking: noun, noun, noun. Sand in the shoe doesn't make you an oyster. This river runs constantly. "The similitude of this great flower," its violent fame. Forfeit your interests while moonlight chucks the sun. Is the dog behind glass, glassed in? Heaven's voice has hell behind it. I'm looking at the evil flower, a fly in the keyhole trying to read the wall. It says we haven't died despite the cold, it sells the green room's sweat and laughter. It's misty in the dream. It says you promised to go on.

In the middle of the brook you surprised me: summer fox, meta-
comet, gingerboy. The point of the story was, does the fox eat the
goose, does the gingerboy melt, can she fly to shore? I'm crawling
toward the corn, kicking open the field. I see the face in flower and
want to draw it, I chop the tree without thinking, a book or a sub-
tle lean-to. What if we were standing by the boat, like Seabiscuit
deciding whether to run the lane or drift into forbidden meadows?
So gods fall to earth with tender irritation. What we love in time
kills us, poppy dear, sugaring our skulls with backward music.

I stain lengthwise all I touch. The world is so touching, seen this way, in fleshtones, aggrieved, gleaming as the lights go out, looking into the crease of relativity. We've seen this before, why? Triumph arches over us like bad emotion. We were supposed to feel more connected to it, we were supposed to feel humanly moved by imaginary strings. All the words in the world are moving pictures to the dizzy ear, fleas, inadequate deceptions of nocturnal hair, pushing buttons, pushing papers, pushing pedals up the long hill. Who could get over the blatant radiance of a name like Doris Day, throwing your finest features into political relief, a warehouse in the shadow of apples and streams?

Infancy moons us with misty cloudcover, an updraft nearly laundered of intent. Palmed and tendered in subaltern shade, I could not shake the memory of a train that whitely striped the hills. The surrendering pike pours out in uniform. Butter-gloved epiphanies slide past us in their muscle car. In the words of the daffodil, am I in my kerchief more lovely than the ash kicking up against the wheel? What form do women take? Or is she taken like a path to frosty metaphor, a seed easier crushed than opened? Can a word be overturned by jest, or does it take a wayward spark to fire up your arsenal of lace? The darkest blue is black, felt around the edges. I give the cool a running start, a catching chance, rigging our descent to decent landings, piloting home.

I came back to the meadow an unsuspecting hart, trying to wake up from a long night of walking. I was looking for a subtext, a heavy horsey bee doing battle with its inclination. What's your angle? A little evanescent on the rim, it's only a willow, beaked and shining, a toothy margin holding up banks. Have we overstayed our party in the heavenly city or are we spilling through its gates trying not to get trampled? On the berm I filled a basket with crashing birds. In the dream you pointed sideways with your thumb where the cars were flying.

Idly I turned your name into a kite. Poor bloom couldn't find itself among the interrupted lady. A little less air for the megaphone, a larger flag over Brownsville. We're knotted in eights at bossomy altitudes, foreshortened in the wind. Feet are but a bit of leather, breaking through the turf. A stroke of sunlight in a wreck of a bedroom, a mirror of temporary verbs. As for the daisy, I know I frighten you. My face a red bookishness. The rose willow produces other kinds of monsters but the imperishable nettle thinks for us all.

While we dug up the garden of western expansion, my witty rope frayed. I was looking for your mitt but now the last grassy shred is about to escort me over the cartoon cliff. If I could only get these eggbeaters to compensate for the anvil foreshortened above my head. I always loved your laugh. I could guess your appetite, arrange my torso like a shield. What's wrong with falling into starry goo or folding flowers against our dizzy inward heights? This is what drives us farther out to sea, to look at our mess beneath the bleach and bluing of some other weather.

A DESCRIPTION OF
THE POISON TREE

The girl is a grid, silked with phenomena, an early promise broken into clover. An owl bends both its eyes to this object. Her desire for shining, a symptom of this bashfulness. Among the lower orders a W is sibilant. A physical lantern, honey in the ear. A larger bird's cry may be hidden from view by a broad enough table. I find her in delirium about to pass for mad. The letter S between the teeth, pushed back into the mouth, as when confronted she has pointed to the word "paper." She doesn't want to be the dollar sign, split and smirking, living in a desert of bolted-down things.

The house of mirth is casting its shadows. My bureau, my agency, a wall of sliding glass. Without its leaky reverie, the face is a shield. Who wouldn't love the sycamore in spite of its skin? For a minute the fountain was an indoor labyrinth, a garden gone wild into perfect order. See the bleeding ankle? The meat of the body left alone to run the house. In the company of A or B, in the company of M or W, unfixed by science, a leaning spectacle. The delicate column, the poppied hill.

Girl is notational, she's an index. From the couch I see Mary say-
ing yes and no, he and she. We're only clay: blossom machines.
Sure I'll carry your latest worry, sorry it's not dripping in your
favorite green. Our cheeks are marked with leafy stains. What lasts
forever won't survive its station any more than that junebug can
translate through the screen. We're living on, anyway, immaculate
lawns. Neo-forsythia.

THIS CIRCUMSTANCE IS
WORTH FURTHER ATTENTION

Pertaining to the current trance, "Who Is Sylvia," and "What Is She that All Swains Adore Her," etc? The dahlia's abundance can't help but fix the room, its lesson of impermanence buried in quikrete. Who is the *maître* of county W? Someone was not meant to be beaten on the road, though the stars declare it. Thinly municipal, we're almost brainless waiting on the curb. A fruitless search at war with forgetfulness. Here is an account of my life as a shipmate, W itself. Sighed upon and sleeved, sighing and sleepy, we turn this observation into continental science, encumbered at the gates, the fires of hazardville smoking up our skirts. The word "delicious" has never been redder, the breath of wolves so hot on our ankles, I think we walk on bloody fire.

The devil's in shirtsleeves, smoking with Vandals. I have the magic nose to make him disappear but in my dream I can't reach it. In my dream robots are picking up garbage and hauling it down the bloc so accurately they seem to be loving us. They are short and pitiful, they are gardening next door. If I could only read their alphabet or learn how to sleep, but I'm roaring like Helen. I can see you in the distance, as if the robots could take me there. As if you're their leader sitting hotly on the wire.

Lost words are lost boys. These woods are combing the hair of paradise. You're waking and thinking, an opera of our minor ways: Sweet William, Virginia. What we fear in fearlessness turns over the table. You don't blame the lamp for what you cannot read, the fire in the match not struck. How many coats, by federal surprise, regard you from the banks? We think we see them through the screen, the darkest flower's gabardine.

VERSES OMITTED.

VERSES OMITTED

Belimbed as a willow
I'm burning with wingedness

Our midnight special
launched toward precipity

Don't let another season
make a joke of piracy

I swim to shore
every day

unfashionably mirrored
with iridescent moss

Even in terror
surely we survive

the scheduled collapse
of yesterday's cakes

CANTO.

ON THE RESEMBLANCE OF
SOME FLOWERS TO INSECTS

A smoky vessel drifts east like a slippery elixir. By simple rotation night collapses with its head in the dirt, though from the heights it appears more like cubist swagger. Suddenly curtains. What lives in a room takes on the spirit of the room. This is true even of television. Imagine deciding the gulley a life will follow as if choosing breakfast over diligent labor. I don't remember my first brush with pollen, yet I've watched words flower sideways across your mouth. In a month we'll be dizzily older. Moths will leave singed paper on the stoop. Is this my design? An ant crosses my shadow so many times looking for its crumb, I think it's me who's needlessly swaying. Its path is busy eloquence while I'm merely armed, like a chair leaving the scent of large things on the breeze.

I thought I was reading but suddenly I'm read. Some kind of artist then, painting his targets. Distinct or indistinct sensation? I prefer clarity when I can afford it. So what if another flower plagiarized the rosary? I'd pick up a dime in private or a quarter in public, money's always been "dirty," some kind of death wish. Sure I'd like to own a pet, not own but take care of, not a monkey or donkey, but something that loves you like money or luck. Not a puppy made of flowers but like music, in dog years.

Such a tree I think is sweeping out this country air, I'm thinking about corruption. Even in the playground there's a less-than-certain wind. All those dancers waiting for the bell. The boy assigned to find the missing ball has climbed my mental fence and isn't leaving. Surely that post was once meant for horses. Something pearl, of underwater stowage. Something clearer beyond the polished glass.

A painted tree shadows the river. In a compound eye, nature leans away from struggle, the name is implied. See how he is taken by one hand, or by his leg, a starry gas beating overhead. From the eastern balcony, horizon blinks like a bug. The paradox of counting spreads its ink across the page, a signature more built than drafted. To see or not see. Do you read or hear it? As if by hunger, earth empties its mind.

OF WHICH I SHALL HAVE
OCCASION TO SPEAK AGAIN

Look at the base, asking to be stolen. Someone in the cash family, staining our hands. Who thought in this idyll we'd be lying on needles? Like what's-her-name in the movie about the doctor, so unlike a shepherd. A loosely valid enterprise, god and his pair of dice. This meadow, I swear, cashes in on leaflessness. We're sliding in the outfield, sure it's alive. I'm drawn to the warmth of what doesn't belong to me, waking up on the bus with money in my pants.

His flying mantle, is it not silk? Do I not eat a sandwich that, by this alias, stands the rain and continues to study my face? Is there not a playwright behind the screen awaiting my emergence? Am I not baffled, as any other fabric? As for knowledge, there is rain and frost. His notion of sky, carried to the edge of Venice. See Ariadne, begin with the horses. What is your tribe and your eminent leafage, your robed rhetorical temperature? Cabbage or ivy or rose.

Silvery measures are being cut down, tricked by sun to slaughter.
My elm won't even let me break a sweat, something to believe
by or just forget the dream, a fiery underlife, my score. My part
becomes a piece of glass, a hand outside, against the one inside it.
Make that ship you're thinking of a ship already, so I'll find it, in
the water, in the sun.

Here's a cloud deciding to decide if nature repeats itself. A form like Saturday, the easiest cloverleaf. A helicopter spectacle stops us in the road. I've lost the face that brought me here, the brush of what I'm brought to hear. If a fox tore my throat, I wouldn't sell it to lead a life of "curable sorrows." Vive la guerre, said the box. Fear companies of righteous thought. The human heart is like a cheese. Still justice may emerge from love, stained with grass, in fiercer neighborhoods.

Scudding past fancy lights, I'm writing toward your face. If pages
enter, they do it with my blessing. There's no limit to the boy car,
its floating night. Noise is noise. Such a you, buying dynamite,
rustling in gauze. Don't speak till sound has eclipsed its idea,
your thoughts are on the phone. Of course I'd like a lake, but do
we need all ten thousand? The mind can fit just one, well placed
among its cabins. How big is our room if we can't see its edges?
Steer that boat toward me like you hope to arrive.

Even sighs cast their stormclouds, rising up the fence. Without his sword the count was only counting with his head on the floor. A dead man with his books. Doors swing like faces between every kind of hopefulness. So like a curtain, I can't even pull the string. By evening we're sewing a new kind of flag. In the muddy face of spring, someone's slinging pretty frosting, fitting our thoughts with pear-like wonder, something to wear like a ladder in your hair.

THE MOST POWERFUL
MACHINE IN THE WORLD

It's later than average, it's mist upon the blog. Let's fog the glass, forget the gallows and the digitized chandelier, the element of wonder. Let's make the emperor cry ink. I want the diamond lane, honey. Soup between the acts. Why Baton Rouge and not Gatorville? "Look the bulb in the eye and you'll be struck off your horse, pretty girl." You can see the mare coming off her track, a smeared face, filled with wild turkey, with southpaw. Why is the key in my hand so hot?

PLANTS POSSESS A VOLUNTARY
POWER OF MOTION

Ham begets Ham. A lithe green patch pitches south, a sunny airport's unthinkable cargo. Enameled and arched, I'd rather be brick. When brick I'd prefer to be swimming. My other car has invisible wings. In the mirrored mirror, a comet trucking. Whenever two upon the dew, the coneflower, a roadside feather. The firefly lingers, deer in the weeds. A little something for the young finch, milky begonias compliant as steel.

Continuing to rise, all that's written is "love," a cracked overture, your physical stitch. It's noticeably colder above the road to self-rule. Even beneath a crayon sun, the bottle tipping into folly. I've never thought to take the stair with anything but twilight. Desire comes to leaf beneath the heel, shine dripping off the engine. Grimed beyond reach, a fire moved beyond your face, all rocket, all flare.

VERSES OMITTED BY MISTAKE.

Were I invited
to draft that flower

an unfixed wilder thing
would fix upon my palm

Those wolves are numbered
to a government rifle

If Lucy rules
the castle of indolence

I joy to dream
a more fortunate planet

CANTO.

PICTURES CONNECTED BY A
SLIGHT FESTOON OF RIBBONS

When the ship is in danger, a bell can be the most familiar sound. Traveling by coach or the disastrous locomotive refinements of wind. Of important motionless conversation, the mouth's wicked noise, an internal sensation of ten and of apparent fever, an alcove of Lear. To voluntarily dissolve before a lesser lens, to bark and blither till the end in drunkenness, or as a cottage trembles above the snow with a surprise like joy.

Dawning at the shoulder, I beg to add this foliage. A butterfly placed to resemble a country. The grove to whom you bring a cloak, the vital air you see through. Not moist or dry, not clay as we know it, her cheek of luxe enamel, colorless glass where the capital has fallen. Accidental arguments, described as mysteries, pull the needle in the dark. The law stands or rests, its fame in flower, its leaf-like warmth. To present a real person, sitting on a book, the torch must be in someone's hand, abandoned to its latitude, hungry of shade.

One person's idyll is another's confinement. Midnight every-
where is praying through the noise, a token of the obvious. Hours
blurt out buds like synonyms of battle. Depending on your sub-
ject, a cup may be a sword, dropped on the tile like a capital "is."
To put away, to be instant, like "the sands of Iwo Jima," an eager
policy toward the nearest sea. Someone dreamed a fire would
quench it, something drew a finger through the fire.

The past torches itself like a mummy, dear but misremembered. What did you manage to remember of your day at the beach, blood in the sand? We're close enough to touch the bull's horn with a gasp. Of course I pity a boy among crows. A spectator trawling for the roundest metaphor to counterweight the stabbing air. What gives, or gave, to get us here, what wired fluorescence? The treelike nerves to become all things. Turned in, reflected, postponed.

Tragedy saunters to the pit, swinging its depth charge. If you had X-ray vision you could watch these bones climbing the Mountain Vainglorious without quite touching the ground. Let's ruin our letters, erase all foreign prospect. So many expeditions are but fictive inflections, the garbled ambition of someone stepping up with, like, something less lovely than the legs of Rome. Thumb-power instead of "timber." The answer from above the stage rattles our windows, a modern letter sent from antiquity, its blurred flourish abundantly gutted.

Let me just say that I'm hanging from this screen into an icy darkness. All this planetary turning on a hinge. My head is fair but plain, thinking of Rutherford. I was looking in the window of a newer Canaan, but the dew on its lilies tasted like salt. This piece of my mind is just beyond the hammering, a dog in the yard drifting like trash. Every season cannot be thought at once, even when the world can name it.

So much for swans. Or, having lost it, "add this city to my weather." Being vernal, I've had it with desire. A winter scene middled and rung, with its brilliant use of stupefaction. Something closer, a less gratuitous tower. Incumbent lilies seem to own their consequence, someone's on her back. What do you think of our soldiers, Elizabeth, trying not to be disappointed? I'm not even parked at the gold-rimmed lake, forget about the china. The body is always softer than its image. Shined up, collectible, all it imagined.

Remembering the weather doesn't mean we make it happen. A king shows up like boredom, almost chic it's so real. Our species puts us down beyond the trees, a colophon for everything that's broken in the grass. Folks pan out like zeroism on the grid, the state is red or blue. Flags are in stitches, factoring out the latest breeze, the "she" of elation. Of further benefit, America owns the moon. Even something simple can be squared to death. Try to scale this pyramid while it's cooking into glass. Prepare yourselves for a rigorous chill, be urgently chiffoned.

We're so close to the ocean I can taste it, like the volcanic in Picasso. A hand can fit perfectly over a mouth. I know about the thighbone, but what's this connected to? A skirt trailing off into scorpion silver at the edge of L.A. Compare this with the habits of the wife of Bath, her passing breezes, the stolen pear, tallied for change, tailed to the last, her little Spanish clock. This star plane is mechanical, it's having us on. What long teeth you have.

As luck conducts the inner man, a trumped up art will fly beneath the wings. A southern trick, a secret in peril. The worldly union of what I know best, the horns of August, the downward tree. Your brass face topples the weight of you, blue on blue. Gorky to Hartigan. The street is for sale. The painted gun that once was flower. The nerve-like system in the page. These thoughts are not descriptive.

DEPARTURE OF THE NYMPHS
LIKE NORTHERN NATIONS
SKATING ON THE ICE

At borders everywhere, this is what we fly with, this poppy I'm pouring, coming down like tar. To wonder if the list is earned, to be looking for an island, just one flowering minute. Some powder I was reaching for floats above my hand. Why not crab the fence when you can find it, why not pose before the fire? I catch the flood with my toe. Flowery carpets floor the idyll. Even if I don't write it down, I'm just a form of tuning. I take this green to build my shirt. I do this work to word you.

Suddenly the daisycutter someone was waiting for. I hear the keys like modern ice on its way to hell. We safecrackers have come here for the job, a gasp among luggage. Useless wings. Hook & eye. Assemblage as forgiveness. Get in the car on collaborative ankles. We're rowing like Greeks before those trees turn to treason, erased of all their writing.

SOLAR VOLCANOS

If I appear to play the violin, it's only to keep my head on. Everything heavy falls in September, a fire truck lost on polar seas. I see the blueness in our thinking, lit up from behind. Turning to salt, turning to stone, I'm turning into water. When my blood plays cold, just think where my face has been. If I can speak for the entire space station I'd say we've suffered less than most. Maybe this moment is a test of coloration, an ashy mountainside made to look like dawn.

ERRATA.

ERRATA

for isle, read isles
for boated, read bloated
for poetry, read poetic
for second, read third
for his, read her

for bursts, read burst
for the, read her
for "departure of the gnomes"
read "transmigration of matter"
for shut, read shuts
for sinking, read shrinking
for frigorific, read frigorescent
for her, read its
for word, read world

CANTO.

LOUD CRACKS FROM
ICE MOUNTAINS EXPLAINED

The alarm in my heart is made of silly brass, some of us can't help but mourn the end of Lorca. Rain continues into rain, fire interrupts my car with all the better reason of the forest. I see misfortune in the eye of real weather. Pronouns understand their game before we join the histories that betray us. The happening of summer, all verb upon the land. Could word belie its little clouds, Montblanc would storm against the poet's skin. His mansion is her excess love, a careful avalanche of we and they. A footstep bound for weary day awaits its sound upon the grain.

WHY NO NEW PLANETS ARE
EJECTED FROM THE SUN

These our ships are the copies of copies. This x is that, lifting off the dock. We think we're here because we're crouching in the umber of syllables, that sun is "killing me," a flag among flies, our frozen boat in frozen oil. Let's haunt the beach instead of this history beset with cosmic jelly. At the blind is it morning already? The word has meant so many things, I need a fence to move this gem-like feeling. Or I'm that bus, in hacked-up disquiet, stuck at the light.

When I crossed the road, I burned with the heat of its traffic. Time as movement, a government of rushes. All those itching satellites, blind among the dreaming guns. A bee in its lace is the author of something. Easy work is out there, just beyond the mines. A cab into heroic legend, the first of its kind. To look back on gasoline as hoof and leaf. A moving eye, scrolling through the weeds. Just another carnivore frozen at the spring. As dirty as heaven, a skeleton key.

"Rabbits on the grass" like "all his good women": an effect like vertigo. When I was a child, the sun was socialism surely on my foot, my heart was made of wine, I dreamt, I still had all of you to spend. A face that can't perceive its window will boycott love for any kind of master. This talking cure will brace the child for government futures, the long walk backward with wings in the sand.

Fluent in applejack, I'm knocked off my horse but gaining on liberty. No one spends all his life tanked, what do I mean "spends"? What do I mean "his"? I'm wiping my face on your sleeve as if I'm looking through my own sun. We live in the flower, so I can't taste anything. It's that hot, Tex, a new kind of glue. O, I think therefore I green the grass I'm pinned upon.

The letter A is so public, it can't be protected. Surely the jonquil is a sign of something. A sky so heavy I can't drive without drowning. Think about grass in the heaviness of dew, it doesn't run away. Sadness, you can see, is attached to my body. Don't delay your concrete resistance even while looking at the face of a daisy. Our boldest type is barely detected, disguised by the habits of first and last things.

Night divides sullenness from sudden exposure, a chill can last so long. I sneak the coolest air into my mouth, surprising your ear with summer shade. The light goes out if I'm less than touching, a fencing term for the intimacy of death. Your mother's on the waterways, even while you sleep. Pumpkin has no faults against azure, coherent as a match. Can't the stew arrange itself, perfectly tempered while the houses come awake, blue beyond reason, re-linquishing their branches?

This is my heart, a bird in the building. So much for paratactic liberation. To make a massacre, a mess of things, I'd say some things are not to be erased. Porridge isn't meant to fly. Elevated dusk-talk sinks us one more time breathlessly. It's some kind of country then, beyond the jurisdiction of anyone's lamplight. I've sharpened this girlishness to saw through the fumes and wonder what happened to my tolerance for heaven.

In defense of earthliness, my mouth fills with bubbles. Couldn't you love me in spite of my predicate? "We worry" about omissions, but haven't we been watermarked, aghast? The truth sells itself to star logic, childless in the house of Becky. I'm tracing these words with vigorous calipers, a gentian oracle, what else? I, important to myself in rattled leaf matters, very laureate in turns, I am almost asleep in it. You, over there, constabular trees. Your hand on my wastedness. Your hand on my stem.

What sudden rhetoric trembles at the door? I see clouds reflected
in the gutter, but they're still clouds. Having never shot a deer, I
ride the hill like homeward ire. Outpaced, unpetaled, a boomer-
ang of star fury: all my busted rigor. Whatever it is arranges itself
for capture, the wormwood box, ghost of a chance. No one's alone
anymore. A name slides home, two words dashed to silly alchemy,
a sun uncorked of glory. What little monster have I made, to favor
love of all that's said?

This dirtball invites me to think "with" not "for" it. I display a desperation spoken straight from my feet. Should I hear you cry, I wouldn't think before I dropped my glove to find you; that's how dirt thinks. Why the ear, the shape of longing, why the endless whorl you came from? Seeing air doesn't mean it sees you back. The latest molecule might travel far enough to hide you underground for good. Even while we stare the season down, worlds pour like symptoms of its greedy polished joy.

This I, this me, I'm speaking from a book. That brain that taught me delicious things, forgivable trains, a signal business. I don't want to be tragic, even to the goldleafed bug. I, Walt Whitman, with Texas in my mouth. Dismiss this fantasy in favor of our startled shade. I remembered my tricks and what they did. Even apples aren't free. Our life against the midnight lens: poor Crusoe on Mars. I'm walking through this wall of air to comfort my senate.

We all live under the rule of Pepsi, by the sanctified waters of an in-ground pond. Moss if it gathers is a sign of shifting weathers, the springing scent of consensual facts. A needle's knowing drops into focus while you sleep in its haystack. A boy on the road, a guileless girl disguised as a brook. Even trees deploy their shadows, embossing your skin with the sound of freedom breaking. No one mistakes choice for necessity. Look at the pilgrims in your filmy basket, illustrious eyebrows colored with chalk. The lake is panicking. A latent mystery detected in sepia is quaking to its end. I too have a family astonished, unsaintly. Asleep, I saw them. A porcelain dome insisting on trust, jeweled with telepathy. I don't know how to pour this country from a thinner vessel. Or account for the era of martian diplomacy. Little bridges connect every century, seasonally covered with the rime of empire. Can you successfully ignore the eyes in the painting? Can you recount the last three images in reverse order? I read the picture and did what it told me, ducking through the brush with my tablet and pen, following some star.

Note on the Text

The muse of this book is Erasmus Darwin, the late eighteenth-century doctor, botanist, inventor, poet, and intellectual precursor to his grandson Charles. The investigative energy and poetic ambition of his *Botanic Garden* (1791) suggested not so much a form as a sensibility with which to approach a period of political, intellectual, and biological transformation. Darwin's poems address everything from the sexual life of plants to the evils of slavery, the conquest of Mexico, Franklin's experiments with electricity, and the relation of poetry to painting. In their unwieldy asymmetries and their sudden leaps between botany, political and aesthetic history, technology, and pastoral romance, this work of the late Enlightenment seemed an eerily apt model for riding out the inter-discursive noise of the early twenty-first century. Poetry, it says, can be at once an account of the physical world, a rethinking of the order of things, and a caprice. Like his contemporary William Blake, Darwin made poems that perform as well as contain their intellectual discoveries. The poems of his *Botanic Garden* are interrupted by prose footnotes, supplementary notes, summary descriptions, errata, and dialogues on the relation between poetry and prose, painting, and music. The prose cantos and lyric interruptions of *Meteoric Flowers* reverse the relation between prose and verse in Darwin's work. In tribute to his influence and his love of conversation, the titles of these poems are drawn from Darwin's text.

Acknowledgments

Thanks to the editors of the journals and anthologies in which some of these poems first appeared: *26*, *Baffling Combustions*, *Canary*, *Chicago Review*, *Conjunctions*, *Crowd*, *Dislocate*, *Explosive*, *The Hat*, *No*, *Open City*, *Sentence*, *TriQuarterly*, *Xantippe*, *Yawp*, and *Walt Whitman Hom(m)age 2005/1855* (Turtle Point Press/editions joca seria).

Thanks to Rod Mengham of Equipage for his production of the limited-edition chapbook entitled *The Great Egg of Night* and to Michael Cross of Atticus/Finch for his production of the limited-edition chapbook entitled *Meteoric Flowers*, both of which included a number of these poems. Additional thanks to the Howard Foundation, the California Arts Council, and the MacDowell Colony for their support of this project.